THE CHURN, COLN AND LEACH VALLEYS
VALLEYS
IN OLD PHOTOGRAPHS

THE CHURN, COLN AND LEACH VALLEYS

IN OLD PHOTOGRAPHS

COLLECTED BY

EDWIN CUSS AND PHILIP GRIFFITHS

ALAN SUTTON

Alan Sutton Publishing Limited
Phoenix Mill · Far Thrupp · Stroud · Gloucestershire

First Published 1990

British Library Cataloguing in Publication Data

Churn, Coln and Leach valleys in old photographs.
1. Gloucestershire, history
I. Cuss, Edwin II. Griffiths, Philip *1926-*
942.41

ISBN 0-86299-854-9

Front Cover Illustration:
THE SWAN HOTEL AT BIBURY, 1904. This hotel was as popular ninety years ago as it is today.
Frank Busby was proprietor of both this hotel and of the Bull Hotel at Fairford and
consequently the fly-fishermen could use either hotel and fishing rights. The horse-drawn
bus which is outside often carried the fishermen between the two hotels.

Typeset in 9/10 Korinna.
Typesetting and origination by
Alan Sutton Publishing Limited.
Printed in Great Britain by
The Bath Press, Avon.

CONTENTS

INTRODUCTION

The rivers Churn, Coln and Leach are three of the tributaries of the River Thames and they all flow in a general south-easterly direction down across the slopes of the Cotswold Hills before joining the River Thames.

The Churn rises at Seven Springs high up in the hills to the south of Cheltenham. The Coln rises close to Brockhampton to the east of Cheltenham, and the Leach rises by Hampnett north-west of Northleach. All three rivers have well-defined valleys before each reaches the flat river plain to enter the Thames. These three valleys play host to many very picturesque and typically Cotswold communities, villages and an occasional larger town, which presented us with an almost insuperable problem when making such a selection of photographs as this: the problem of attempting to portray the beauty of them all. The whole area is now well explored by tourists who are able to follow each valley fairly easily, but we hope that this selection of photographs will encourage local people to go and look more deeply at what may be on their doorsteps, or at what may be new territory to tourists in the area.

We have endeavoured to include old photographs of each village in each valley and we have shown each valley by proceeding from the river source down to its junction with the River Thames, as this seemed the most logical way. The Churn runs for some twenty miles, the Coln runs for about twenty-five miles and the Leach for about seventeen miles. There are inevitably gaps where no suitable photographs could be found and we have also included more photographs where we considered that the village deserved it or that the community was larger. We are aware that there may not be a great many action photographs for some of the smaller villages, but again this is unavoidable and in these cases we have included general views.

The captions have sometimes given us considerable trouble and we hope that what we have said is correct, but if there are any mistakes then we hope that readers will contact us and help to put things right.

Readers of this book may like to be reminded of similar publications in this Old Photograph Series that contain more pictures of some of the areas covered in this book. These are:

Fairford and Lechlade by Edwin Cuss and Brian Rushby;
Cirencester by Jean Welsford;
Northleach to Stow-on-the-Wold by David Viner;
Stroudwater and Thames & Severn Canals by Edwin Cuss and Stanley Gardiner.

Edwin Cuss, Cirencester
Philip Griffiths, Cirencester

The Churn Valley Villages

SEVEN SPRINGS, C. 1900 This is the source of the River Churn, where seven small springs emerge from the rocks just off the A436 at the crossing of the road from Cirencester to Cheltenham with the road from Birdlip to Andoversford. It is claimed by some people to be the highest source of the River Thames, and no doubt this argument will last for ever. It became a favourite spot for posing for photographs.

CUBBERLEY MILL, C. 1910. About one mile down from the source of the Churn lies the small village of Coberley (also spelt Cubberley). The church of St Giles can be seen to the left. The church has fourteenth-century remains although it was restored in the 1870s. The manor house that once stood close by was demolished in the eighteenth century. This mill was the first one on the small River Churn and is thought to date from the seventeenth century. In 1919 the Wilson family were millers of corn here, but when it fell out of use, the mill was converted into a house in the 1930s.

COLESBOURNE INN, C. 1910. Built in 1827 shortly after the turnpike road was opened, it has a distinctive style with three gables and stone mullioned windows. The attached stable block to the left with its strange shaped windows has now been converted to a restaurant and the whole complex is much altered. It appears that petrol was being supplied at the inn by Alf Miles Ltd, Cheltenham.

COLESBOURNE HOUSE AND CHURCH, 1909. The house was built in 1854 by David Brandon, and at the time of this view it was the home of Henry Elwes who stocked the surrounding parkland with rare trees that he brought back from aboard. The small River Churn fills the ornamental lake by the bridge. The house was partly demolished in the mid-1960s and rebuilt in a smaller form. The church of St James seen through the trees on the left has a fine Perpendicular-style tower and thirteenth-century remains, but was restored in the nineteenth century, also by David Brandon.

COLESBOURNE POST OFFICE, RECTORY AND SCHOOL, c. 1910. This is a typical small village post office set up in a house, with the rectory on the right and the National School of 1851, with its bellcote also designed by Brandon, at the far end. The school closed in 1965 and is now the village hall.

RENDCOMB HOUSE AND CHURCH, 1909. The house in the park was built in the Italianate style in 1863 by Philip Hardwick for Sir F.H. Goldsmid on the site of the old house of Sir Edmund Tame. The Perpendicular-style church of St Peter on the right was rebuilt in the sixteenth century by the Tames and it underwent further restoration in the late Victorian period.

RENDCOMB PARK, 1908. A meet of the Cotswold Hunt at the park has attracted a few followers. The hunt was probably through the grounds of the park.

THE PARK LAKE, C. 1905. The ornamental lake complete with its boat house on the right was fed by the River Churn, but it is now silted up and overgrown.

THE CONSERVATORY OF RENDCOMB PARK, 1907. A typical large Edwardian conservatory with palm trees in stone urns, and a proud head gardener posing in the centre.

Rendcombe Park Stables.

THE PARK STABLES, 1917. The big stable block for the horses of Park House was also built by Hardwick on a four-square pattern with a French-style tower which had two clocks. On the right is the entrance into the estate gardens.

RENDCOMB COLLEGE, C. 1930. Park House was converted to a boys school, founded by F.N.H. Wills, in 1920. This picture clearly shows the symmetrical three-storeyed building and the tall Italianate tower with its hipped roof. The classrooms were on the ground floor and the dormitories were on the two upper floors.

RENDCOMB VILLAGE, 1912.

RENDCOMB VILLAGE, C. 1910. In the top view are the blocks of cottages built by Hardwick which are quite alien to the local Cotswold style, especially with their patterned tiled roofs. On the left is the blacksmith's forge and farm implements can be seen behind the wall awaiting repair. In the lower view is the track from the lower part of the village up to the Park Drive.

WOODMANCOTE, c. 1920. This is a small hamlet and once again the cottages on the left were designed by Hardwick in 1865 for Sir F.H. Goldsmid, while other cottages around were of the Cotswold style. There is also a seventeenth-century manor house in the village.

Burcomb Woodmancote, Cirencester   No. 5715

WOODMANCOTE, c. 1960. This is not strictly an old photograph but it shows the newly opened modern-style housing built at the top end of the village.

THE BATHURST ARMS, NORTH CERNEY, C. 1910. This view is looking up the hill into the village across the bridge over the river. This public house with its gardens set alongside the River Churn is still very popular.

NORTH CERNEY VILLAGE, C. 1910. This view is looking through the village with the new post office on the left and a well-posed group of children in the road. A row of telegraph poles comes through the village but there is only one line on them.

NORTH CERNEY CHURCH, c. 1915.

NORTH CERNEY VILLAGE, c. 1915. In the top view is the church of All Saints. It was started in the twelfth century and has been altered over the centuries but has been well restored due to the generosity of Mr W.I. Croome. The lower picture looks across the village from the churchyard. The main road from Cirencester to Cheltenham runs across the foreground with the large manor in the centre. In front of the manor is North Cerney Mill, the machinery from which was taken to Arlington Mill in 1966.

North Cerney House.

NORTH CERNEY HOUSE, C. 1915. This is basically a seventeenth-century house with a Georgian rebuild after a bad fire. It is set on the western side of the valley up the hill beyond the church. Behind the house are the Scrubditch Iron-Age ditches associated with the Belgic Dobunni settlement at Bagendon.

Badgendon Church, Glos.

BAGENDON, C. 1915. This hamlet lies on a small tributary of the Churn, and the church of St Margaret has a saddle-back tower and dates back to Norman times. South-east of the hamlet are the remains of the dykes that enclosed the 200-acre site of the capital of the Dobunni. These people were well established here prior to the Romans coming and the site included a mint and other metal-working activities. The site was excavated in the mid-1950s. Note also the manor house to the right.

Baunton Church.

BAUNTON CHURCH, C. 1915.

A Peep in Baunton. April 25th., 1908

A PEEP IN BAUNTON, 1908. This is a typical W.D. Moss postcard with a typical caption by him, which was used many times. The scene is of the heavy snowfall on 25 April, which was followed by a quick thaw. It is thought that this lane is the one that leads on from the dead-end road by the church and which follows the valley up to Perrots Brook.

BAUNTON MILL, 1909. The Mill House and the Mill were at the bottom of the steep hill down into the village from the main road. This winter scene shows the mill building to the left. Using both water and steam power, Walter Hayward was miller here in 1919.

Baunton Church & Part of Village.

BAUNTON CHURCH AND VILLAGE, C. 1915. The church of St Mary Magdalene and the village lie away from the main Cheltenham road and this view shows the Norman church which was restored in 1877 when a fourteenth-century wall painting of St Christopher was uncovered. The Churn lies over to the left in water meadows.

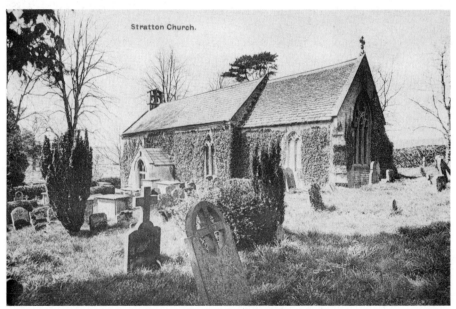

Stratton Church.

STRATTON CHURCH, C. 1910. The small church of St Peter has Norman remains but was restored in 1850. The Grange next to the church has some good farm buildings.

STRATTON GARAGE, 1980. This is not an old photograph but the 1930s-style building has now been demolished and replaced with a modern garage and petrol station.

GOOSEACRE LANE, c. 1920. Almost into Cirencester along the main Abbey Way road, this little lane leads through to Gloucester Street with a bridge over the River Churn. The sheds over to the left are the Bridges / A. Rees workshops and there was a coal yard in later years immediately over the bridge.

MARKET PLACE, C. 1900. The fifteenth-century church of St John Baptist and the old town hall dominate the scene. The church with its fine perpendicular tower was restored in 1865–67 by Sir G.G. Scott. There are no cars to be seen and very few people either. Note the ornate street lamps, especially the one by the horse trough in the centre.

MARKET PLACE, C. 1930. As we look towards the south side away from the church the dignified frontage of the Kings Head Hotel dominates the scene. The Market Place now has all the makings of a good traffic jam with cars and buses going in all directions. There is only one horse present on the left.

F.W. MOODY SHOP, C. 1905. There is a fine display of game and fish at the shop at No. 17 Market Place. It is probably Mr Moody standing in the doorway with the delivery boy, and the two aproned assistants standing by the side entrance.

EMPIRE DAY, 1906. This occasion was always celebrated around the villages and mainly in the schools, but a more stylish affair was celebrated in the Market Place of Cirencester with a military parade and flags flying from the shop windows. The National Anthem and various other patriotic songs were sung.

The Abbey, Cirencester

THE ABBEY HOUSE, C. 1915. Built in 1776 on the site of an old manor house, this was the seat of the Chester-Master family. It was demolished in the 1960s and replaced with a block of flats which is still called Abbey House. The Norman gateway and arch on the main road are all that remain of the original Augustinian Abbey which stood on this site. The Master and Chester-Master family lived here for four centuries.

THE ABBEY HOUSE ORNAMENTAL LAKE, C. 1920. The waters of the Churn divide and one part fills this lake and the other passes close alongside the main road over to the left outside the line of the Roman wall around Corinium. The bank in the background represents the remains of that wall at this point. The meadows by the lake were used for cattle grazing and were also cut for hay, but they are now a public park called the Abbey Grounds.

THE GWR STATION CORNER, 1909. Four roads meet here, Castle Street, Sheep Street, Tetbury Road and Park Lane. The GWR branch-line terminus was behind the railings having reached the town in 1841 from the main line at Kemble. It was closed to passengers in 1964 but the Brunel-designed station building still survives in the centre of the car-park site.

CIRENCESTER FROM THE TETBURY ROAD, C. 1925. The approach down Tetbury Hill into the town is almost unchanged today with the former police station, built in 1859, in the centre and the Marlborough Arms on the corner to the right. On the left is the high wall of the park, and the former Museum of Roman Antiquities which was opened in 1856.

PARK STREET, C. 1910. Outside Perrett's bakers shop is a GWR delivery horse and cart. This building is now the Corinium Museum which also incorporates the eighteenth-century Abberley House next to it. The road turns left into Black Jack Street or right into Silver Street and on the corner are the Victorian redevelopment buildings in this area of the town.

Picture House and Theatre, Cirencester.

THE OLD PICTURE HOUSE AND THEATRE, 1932. At the junction of Victoria Road and London Road the Picture House, later to be the Gaumont, is showing *Red Hot Riley* starring George Sidney. The building was demolished in the mid-1960s and a block of flats called Bravender House built in its place.

LONDON ROAD, 1911. The picture house shown in the previous photograph has not yet been built which enables us to see the carriage works of F.W. Constable on the right. By the small cart opposite is the eighteenth-century Oxford House, and the two branches of the river cross underneath the road by the trees.

QUERNS LANE, c. 1900. Looking west from the Sheep Street junction, close to the terminal basin and wharf of the Thames & Severn Canal off to the right.

THE MIDLAND AND SOUTH WESTERN JUNCTION RAILWAY STATION AT WATERMOOR, c. 1900. The line here came from Swindon through to Andoversford and was one of the few railway lines aligned north and south in this part of the country. It was completed to Cirencester in 1883 and finally closed in 1961 and the station and associated yards have now all gone. These yards had workshops for locomotives and carriages, etc. and employed a large number of people, most of whom lived in railway houses in the Watermoor area.

WATERMOOR ROAD, c. 1940. A wartime parade coming up the road towards the Market Place, but what was the occasion?

VICTORIA ROAD, c. 1910. Victoria Road was originally laid out in 1859 and called New Road, but was renamed in 1887 to mark the Golden Jubilee of Queen Victoria. This picture shows the whole length of the road from the corner of Queen Street. A coal cart is delivering bushel baskets of coal to Andrews Bakery on the corner. The Grammar School buildings of 1880 are up past the trees on the right.

VIEW ACROSS VICTORIA ROAD, C. 1880. In the centre is the Talbot Inn and the road runs across the picture with only the houses on the west side built so far. It is taken from the City Bank looking west over what are now the playing fields of the old Grammar School and the end of Purley Road.

RED CROSS HOSPITAL, c. 1915. The Bingham Hall was built in 1908 and the interior is easily recognized here. During the First World War the Hall was taken over for use as a hospital. Note the medicine trolley, the matron's desk and the grand piano in the centre for entertainment. The beds were kept level on the sloping floor by using blocks of wood under the legs. Many hundreds of soldiers were treated here.

THE HIGH SCHOOL, 1904. The Cirencester Girls' High School was founded in 1901 in the Avenue but in 1904 moved down to a new wing of the Grammar School in Victoria Road.

Council Schools, Cirencester.

11.

COUNCIL SCHOOLS, 1909. A boys' school, a girls' school and a mixed infants' school were opened in Lewis Lane in 1879 in these new buildings, which all survive today and are still in educational use.

W.G. BRIDGES, 1911. A garage was started by W.G. Bridges at the Whiteway Works in Spitalgate Lane. Repairs were carried out, accumulators recharged, petrol, oil, grease and motor accessories were sold and cars could be also be hired. Perhaps this chauffeur-driven car is typical of those that could be hired.

AUBREY REES AGRICULTURAL ENGINEERING WORKS, 1975. Following the Bridges concern a large agricultural engineering business occupied the site. Once familiar to many people it is now all gone and Ashley House and the St John's Meadow development fills the area.

AEROPLANE CRASH, C. 1915. During the First World War a biplane crashed near to the town, thought to be in the Tar Barrow field, while attempting to land. The considerable damage is being assessed by two high-ranking officers.

HOUNDS EXERCISING, c. 1935. The V.W.H. (Earl Bathurst's) hounds were kept at their kennels in Cirencester Park. After exercising they are returning to the park up Kill Devil Hill just past the Royal Agricultural College on the Stroud Road. This road was established in 1814 when the old road to Stroud across the park was closed.

YEOMANRY CHURCH PARADE, c. 1915. Companies of the Warwickshire Yeomanry who were camped in the park are assembled on parade for a service in Cirencester Park. The padre and the band are standing by Queen Anne's Monument, a Doric column with a statue of the Queen at the top, erected in 1741.

A GROUP AT ALFRED'S HALL, C. 1910.

INTERIOR OF ALFRED'S HALL, C. 1910. The first Earl Bathurst built various follies in the park and this castellated hall of 1721 is the earliest and the most interesting. The folly was used for all types of events such as concerts and parties and in the top view is a group standing outside the hall while the lower view shows the interior. Today this building survives as a ruin.

VISIT OF MRS PANKHURST, 1911. Women's suffrage aroused considerable interest in the town through the Women's Unionists and the Women's Liberal Association. Mrs Pankhurst visited the town to address a meeting and is seen here with other suffragettes at the top of Cecily Hill.

CHURCH LADS' BRIGADE, 1909. The Cirencester group are seen here in the Abbey Grounds 'trooping the colours'.

RADIO SOCIETY, 1925. Enthusiasts of the Radio Society visited the Leafield Radio Station which was on the high ground by Shipton-under-Wychwood.

The Croquet Club, Chesterville School, Cirencester.

THE CROQUET CLUB, 1904. This club belonged to Chesterville School in Lewis Lane. The school later moved to a house at the old junction of Querns Lane and Querns Hill.

A Peep in Preston.

PRESTON VILLAGE, c. 1905. A view along the road through the village, almost unchanged to this day.

A Peep from the Cricklade Road.

THE RIVER CHURN AT PRESTON, 1906. Again, virtually unchanged as this road, built along the line of Ermin Street, is now no longer used as all the traffic goes along the bypass over to the right. The river goes underneath the bridge to Preston Mill, now a fish farm.

Preston Church.

PRESTON CHURCH, C. 1920. The church of All Saints is mostly Early English but was restored in 1862. It has a fine fourteenth-century bellcote.

SIDDINGTON CHURCH, C. 1905. St Peter's church has good Norman remains and was restored in 1864 when the spire was added. Church Farm almost surrounds the church and in this picture the fine barn is being re-roofed.

THE GREYHOUND, SIDDINGTON, C. 1930. The two horses wait patiently by the side of the road. Note the set of mounting steps by the wall and in the background the slight hump in the road of the bridge over the canal at the bottom of the flight of the four Siddington locks.

Barton Farm, Siddington.

BARTON FARM, UPPER SIDDINGTON, C. 1905. The farm stands at the top of the lane that leads down to the school and the Old Rectory.

UPPER SIDDINGTON LOCKS, 1922. The Thames & Severn Canal came down through four locks off its summit level. Through Overtown Bridge is the top lock, beyond which was the short branch line of the canal into Cirencester. The Canal House, just visible over the bridge, was the headquarters of the eastern end of the canal which was officially abandoned in 1927 although it had not been used since 1911. In this picture there is no water and the bottom gates have collapsed.

SIDDINGTON ROUNDHOUSE, 1931. This eighteenth-century castellated roundhouse stands on rising ground between Siddington and South Cerney. Perhaps built as a folly or as a windmill, it was used as a house for many years.

THE COLLEGE, 1907. Founded in 1834 by Anne Edwards it was a home for clergy widows. Built in a Tudor-Gothic style it was not at all in keeping with the Cotswold style of the rest of the village at that time.

ATKYNS MANOR HOUSE, C. 1910. A fine seventeenth-century Cotswold-style gabled house, clearly showing the extended left-hand side. The garden at the rear has an interesting gazebo alongside the River Churn.

THE LOWER MILL, C. 1910. This view is looking down Bow-Wow with the long and narrow mill pond, for the two water wheels in the mill, on the right. The mill is most probably taking the majority of the water here as there appears to be very little in the River Churn on the left.

SCHOOL LANE, 1909. A marvellous village scene with the school just off the picture on the right and the blacksmith standing outside the forge with machinery for repair. The present village hall is now where the buttressed and thatched barn is on the right.

THE VILLAGE CROSS, C. 1910. This cross with its stone ball and iron cross was at the centre of the village and the two carts are in Clarks Hay, the road to Cirencester. The buildings have had alterations but the scene is otherwise much the same.

THE HIGH STREET, 1910. Looking back up the street with the Royal Oak on the right. Across the ditch on the left now stand the houses built in the 1930s. The small cottages in the centre have also gone.

THE VILLAGE CROSS AND HIGH STREET, 1911. Another good village scene with two men breaking stone to mend the road and a policeman standing in the picture by the cross. The ditch down the side of the High Street can be seen with the bridges over to the houses while in the centre right, the white-painted building is the Butchers' Arms.

SOUTH CERNEY STATION, c. 1910. The station master of this rural station on the MSWJ Railway stands on the platform as a train from Cirencester approaches. In the background is Bow-Wow Lane bridge with the River Churn crossing under the lines between the bridge and the station. Note the small gravel pit over to the right, some indication of the future as now the whole scene behind the camera position is a large expanse of water left from gravel extraction.

STATION ROAD, 1906. Looking up Station Road towards the cross with the small gabled sixteenth- and seventeenth-century cottages lining the road on the left. As in School Lane, note the thatched roofs.

WILDMOORWAY LOCK, C. 1900. This was a deep lock on the Thames & Severn Canal where a side pond was necessary to help to conserve water supplies. The lock cottage was built sometime after the canal was opened so that the lengthsman transferred from Cerney Wick could be based here to control the lock. The cottage was built into the canal bank with storage underground and then two-up-two-down accommodation. It is now almost completely fallen down, but the site is easily reached from the Spine Road Information Point.

CERNEY WICK LOCK AND ROUNDHOUSE, c. 1904. This picture taken after the GCC restoration of the canal shows the lock chamber and the Round House, originally one of five such buildings along the canal for lengthsmen. At this small wharf goods were loaded and unloaded while the barge was in the lock chamber. A great deal of restoration work has been carried out here by the Stroudwater, Thames & Severn Canal Trust and recently a new pair of top gates were fitted to the lock, which is now in a good state of repair.

Latton Church.

LATTON CHURCH, 1908. The church of St John the Baptist has some Norman remains, especially in the lower part of the tower.

LATTON BASIN AND CANAL JUNCTION, C. 1895. This picture is taken from the towpath bridge over the link between the Thames & Severn Canal and the North Wilts. Canal. This large basin was built at the junction with a toll house and a stop lock leading off into the North Wilts. Canal which joined the Wilts. and Berks. Canal at Swindon. One gate of the stop lock belonged to each canal company so that water could be controlled by whoever had the greatest depth of water here.

LATTON BASIN LOCK-KEEPER, 1918. Mr Alfred Howse was the last keeper at the basin and he worked a small market garden alongside the toll house and used his donkey cart to take the produce to the local markets.

St. Mary's Church, Cricklade.

ST MARY'S CHURCH, C. 1920. The church is thought to have been built in the twelfth century but has been altered a great deal. It was used until 1981 when it was declared redundant. In 1984 it was handed over to the Roman Catholic community and is now regularly used once again.

THE GIRLS' SCHOOL AND PRIORY, c. 1905.

THE PRIORY, c. 1930. In these two similar views the top one shows the school as it was originally built with its bell tower, the Crimean Gun and the Priory in the centre. This was founded in 1231 to provide food and shelter for travellers. The town bridge is just this side of the Priory. The war memorial now takes the place of the gun while the lower view shows that the school has been enlarged.

HIGH STREET, 1908. Taken after the late snowfall of 25 April, this view is looking down the High Street towards Cirencester with the King's Head Inn on the left and the cast-iron jubilee clock erected for Queen Victoria's Diamond Jubilee in 1897 at the crossroads in the centre.

CRICKLADE CHURCH, C. 1920. The large tower of St Sampson's church dominates the district and is a distinctive landmark in the flat countryside. The church was built in the thirteenth century and the tower was added in the sixteenth century. It was restored in 1864. In the foreground is the Market Cross which was removed from the crossroads to the churchyard in 1820.

HATCHETT'S FORD, 1907.

BAPTISM IN THE RIVER THAMES AT HATCHETT'S, 1890. The ford and footbridge are just below the junction of the Churn with the Thames and just outside the old Saxon walls of the town. In the lower view Mrs Freeth is being baptized. It was the last Baptist baptism in the River Thames.

VIEW FROM THE CHURCH TOWER, 1905. This is looking north-west towards Cirencester over the roofs of the houses in Bath Road and the High Street. Many of these roofs have changed but the original layout of the properties in the High Street can be seen with their long plots of ground.

CRICKLADE CEMETERY, 1906. The burial ground and the small chapel were laid out in late Victorian times in the Bath Road. The town received an Order in Council from the Queen to use this new cemetery and not those attached to the churches.

THE BATH ROAD, 1919. This rural scene is along the road out of Cricklade which went on to Malmesbury and eventually to Bath, with the church tower in the distance on the right.

The Coln Valley Villages

BROCKHAMPTON, c. 1910. In this high Cotswold watershed country the River Coln rises to the left in the valley north of the village and flows southwards, while the River Isborn, rising by Charlton Abbots one mile to the north, flows northwards to the River Avon. The village had its own brewery and its chimney can be seen in the centre. It was used for grain drying after the last war.

SEVENHAMPTON, c. 1930, from high in the hills, looking across the valley to the small community. Sevenhampton has many good stone-built cottages with the tythe barn to the right now converted into a house. Brockhampton village is just higher up to the left.

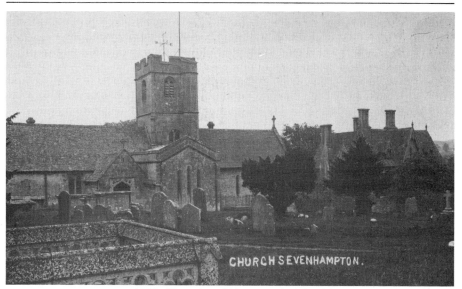

SEVENHAMPTON CHURCH, c. 1935. The original Norman church of St Andrew was altered by John Camber, a wealthy wool merchant of the late fifteenth century, and the central tower required flying buttresses inside the church. The vicarage built in the mid-nineteenth century in the Tudor-Gothic style is to the right.

SYREFORD MILL POND, c. 1930. One mile further south the river flows alongside the mill pond by the road to Syreford Mill which is over four hundred years old. Some years ago water from this lake was used for the local supply. Many years ago excavations near the village revealed a Roman settlement and a fine statuette of Mars was discovered.

ANDOVERSFORD FROM THE GWR STATION, C. 1900. This view is from the end of the platform looking towards the village along the road that later became the A40. The present A40 now bypasses the village using the railway tracks closed in 1962 off to the left. In the centre by the trees can be seen the Andoversford Hotel with the market pens for animals laid out in front of the trees. Much of this village owes its origins to the building of the railway.

ANDOVERSFORD AMATEUR FOOTBALL CLUB, 1922/3. The club was in the final of the Northleach Hospital Cup and this shows the eleven players seated at the front with some supporters and club officials standing at the rear.

THE MILL INN, WITHINGTON, C. 1925. To most people Withington means the Mill Inn which has been a popular hostelry for many years. It is seen here from the western valley slope with the pond in the foreground, the river coming under the road and the valley curling off down to the right. Parts of the inn were rebuilt c. 1960 with old stone from Northleach prison. The Jubilee Hall now occupies a site in the old railway cutting at the top.

WITHINGTON FLOWER AND HORSE SHOW, 1923. A typical village show with the flower show held in the tents, an amusement fair to the left, horse jumping events in the ring and the horse show mainly made up by the local farm carters with decorated carts and horses and freshly painted wagons. The small river is in the bottom of the valley and the picture is taken from the MSWJ Railway.

WITHINGTON HIGH STREET, C. 1925. The church tower of St Michael shows above the houses. The interior was over-restored in mid-Victorian times but it contains a fine monument to Sir John and Lady Howe and their eight children from nearby Cassey Compton.

WITHINGTON VILLAGE CORNER, C. 1925. The house on the right is the School House with a sign to Chedworth Roman villa straight on. To the right past the school is the road to Chedworth village, while the church is immediately to the left. It is a very much busier corner today.

COMPTON ABDALE CROCODILE SPRING, C. 1920. This village is not on the River Coln, but tucked into the steep bank below the church is a stone water trough into which water from the stone crocodile gushes. It overflows and runs down the side of the road to the south to join the Coln at Cassey Compton. There are many springs around the village that are thrown out across the underlying Fullers Earth.

COMPTON ABDALE, c. 1930. A view looking north-west across Lower Farm and part of the village towards the higher ground and the A40 road. The church of St Oswald with its perpendicular and gargoyled tower lies behind the trees to the left. A Roman villa was discovered in the woods at Compton Grove to the west and it was excavated by boys from Cheltenham Grammar School in 1930.

COMPTON ABDALE POST OFFICE, 1916. This was Manor Farm House set low in the ground on the corner opposite the church and crocodile spring. Most likely the ground was made up to stop the road being so boggy. The road runs to Withington with the small stream from the spring alongside it.

COMPTON ABDALE, 1916. This view along the street shows the grocers shop to be one of the focal points of the village. The shop was owned by Mr Pitman who was licensed to sell cider and perry. All the thatched buildings here have now gone.

CHEDWORTH ROMAN VILLA, 1904.

CHEDWORTH ROMAN VILLA, 1935. Two general views showing the excavated site of the villa, which was built between the second and fourth centuries. It was discovered in 1864 and is now recognized as one of the finest in Britain, and it has been owned and administered by the National Trust since 1924. The top view is across the central courtyard towards the north wing of the villa with the bath suites and mosaics protected by sheds on the left, while the lower view is along the north wing with the remains of a colonnade in the foreground. The bank at the rear was cleared of trees in 1933.

CHEDWORTH VILLAGE, C. 1905. This view is looking north-west across Queen Street, with the MSWJ Railway running left to right. The railway was closed in September 1961 but the bridge was only demolished in recent years. The church of St Andrew is at the top right and Manor Farm to the top left. At the end of the central row of cottages is a small shed roofed with the very large stone tiles known as planks.

UPPER CHEDWORTH, 1925. The village pub is the Seven Tuns Inn, shown here at the end of Church Row cottages. The village is not on the River Coln but on a small tributary which rises in the village opposite the inn and leads down almost two miles to the Coln at Fossebridge.

UPPER CHEDWORTH, 1925. This view shows the double track railway line and the entrance to Chedworth Tunnel in the centre. The railway line cut this large village into two parts linked by the road under a tall bridge.

CLUB DAY, C. 1905. More correctly the club was the Chedworth Union Friendly Society who met annually during Easter week. Members and their families paraded around the village starting from the church approach and ending up at the Seven Tuns for a feast. The parade was headed by the Chedworth band and the members carried their club banners which are seen here blowing in the wind.

YANWORTH CHURCH, C. 1910. The small community of Yanworth is on the opposite side of the valley to Chedworth and again is not on the river. The church of St Michael lies among farm buildings but inside the remaining traces of wall paintings are most interesting. On the north side of the church is an enclosure where six Roundhead soldiers were buried following the end of the Civil War.

YANWORTH, 1930. These estate cottages were built in the 1860s by Lord Eldon who then owned Stowell Park Estate. The village post office, with the public telephone, was in the last cottage on the left through the small gate. This remains very much an estate village today.

STOWELL PARK, C. 1910. The Elizabethan mansion house is surrounded by its own park and the twelfth-century church of St Leonard is set within the estate. Various alterations were carried out at the mansion in the mid-1890s for Lord Eldon and more recently the left gabled end of the house shown here has been modified.

THE 160TH US ARMY HOSPITAL AT STOWELL PARK, 1944. This temporary wartime hospital was built in 1942/3 by contractors Percy Bilton for the casualties that were anticipated from the second front after the D-Day landings in 1944. After the war it was partly used as a Polish Resettlement Centre and then as a school. This view is taken looking towards Fossebridge with the main road behind the trees to the left.

FOSSEBRIDGE HILL, C. 1925. Looking north this shows the steep valley of the Coln with the Fossebridge Hotel and community at the bottom of the valley where the Fosse Way crosses the river. Road repairs are being made part of the way down the hill by the Yanworth turning. The road down the hill and up out of the valley to Northleach is very steep and is now much widened for modern traffic.

FOSSEBRIDGE HOTEL, C. 1925.

FOSSEBRIDGE HOTEL, C. 1925. Many alterations and additions have been made to these buildings and it is thought that Lord Eldon lived here while alterations were made at Stowell Park. In the top view the hotel was always a convenient stopping place along the road from Cirencester to Northleach and BP petrol was available for cars in the early motoring days. In the lower view the Coln can be seen coming through the double-arched bridge under the road and flowing down the valley towards Coln St Dennis. Most probably there was a ford here in Roman times.

THE YANWORTH ROAD AT FOSSEBRIDGE, 1912. This small road runs up the valley towards Yanworth and the horse is standing by the blacksmith's shop. Interestingly, all the buildings in this group are thatched, which was much more common on the Cotswolds then than it is today.

THE CHURCH. COLNE ST DENIS.

COLN ST DENNIS CHURCH, c. 1910. This small church retains its plan and much original Norman work apart from the obvious top stage to the tower which was added in the fifteenth century. The ancient village cross seen through the gateway was restored in 1901 in memory of Queen Victoria.

CALCOT, c. 1935. This view of the hamlet shows it set up on the eastern slope of the valley and it remains a quiet and almost untouched village with some seventeenth-century cottages and barns along the street.

COLN ROGERS, C. 1930. This Old Rectory house is opposite Glebe House in the lane that leads down to the church. The valley widens out here sufficiently for watermeadows alongside the river.

COLN ROGERS CHURCH, 1928. This small church of St Andrew still retains a good deal of Saxon work and is unique in this area. It is set well back from the road into the fields and farm. The Saxon work shows most clearly in the long and short quoins and pilaster strips outside, and the chancel arch stonework and small, single, pierced stone windows inside.

WINSON, C. 1920. A beautiful view across the village to the little Norman church of St Michael, set among farm buildings and the eighteenth-century manor house.

WINSON CHAPEL, C. 1900. The small corrugated-iron chapel is now gone but this picture shows a group of elders seated in the centre of a large gathering of about a hundred people from the surrounding district.

ABLINGTON, c. 1910. This view across the hamlet echoes the words used by J. Arthur Gibbs in his book *A Cotswold Village* where he describes it as 'a small village nestling amid a wealth of stately trees.' Ablington is blessed with a good sixteenth-century manor house and some well-built eighteenth-century barns.

ABLINGTON ROAD TOWARDS BIBURY, 1908. With the road dropping down to Bibury the river divides, with the main flow going to Arlington Mill and the river course following the road round in front of the Swan Hotel seen here in the centre. The meadows to the right are now all occupied by the Bibury Trout Farm.

THE CATHERINE WHEEL AT ARLINGTON, C. 1925. The road from Cirencester and Barnsley drops down this hill through Arlington, over the river and into Bibury. The landlord of the pub which was part of the Cirencester Brewery chain, stands proudly in the gateway.

ARLINGTON HILL, C. 1905. Below the Catherine Wheel is the fine sixteenth- and seventeenth-century Arlington Manor House. Note the oil lamp on the street corner. These were indeed unhurried days compared with the crowded tourist streets of today.

ARLINGTON MILL, C. 1955. This is not a very old photograph but it shows what concessions have now been made to tourism. The gardens in the foreground belong to the Swan Hotel but the area between them and the seventeenth-century mill, which is now a museum, is all taken up with the trout farm complex, while across the road a car park has been built. The mill was originally used for both wool and corn and has been altered many times and strengthened both inside and outside.

ARLINGTON ROW, C. 1948. To most tourists this is Bibury, and it must represent one of the most photographed locations in the Cotswolds. The row of cottages is now owned by the National Trust along with Rack Island in front of them, and they are thought to date back to the fourteenth century when they may have been a long barn or wool warehouse. Some new gables have been added in the past but they are now in very good condition.

ARLINGTON ROW, C. 1925. Looking down the row from the steep roadway known as Awkward Hill, or more locally as 'Okerd ill'. The small stream that runs in front of the cottages is the tail race out of Arlington Mill across the other side of Rack Island.

THE STREET, BIBURY, 1903. The river is some thirty feet wide here and is spanned by the three-arched stone bridge which carries the road from Cirencester. The three horse carts and the one Edwardian lady offer a complete contrast to the modern scene here today. It is interesting to note that the river is very low and almost choked with weeds.

ALONG THE RIVER COLN, 1912. This view to the south-east, down the river in the opposite direction to the previous picture, shows Rack Island and a glimpse of Arlington Row through the trees to the right.

THE STREET, BIBURY, C. 1900. At this end of The Street there were always a few small shops and prominent here is the shop of 'Morris, Makers of Saddles and Harness, Cirencester', a typical village business.

THE SQUARE, BIBURY, 1913.

THE SQUARE, BIBURY, C. 1905. The village centres around The Square to the north-west of the church with seventeenth- and eighteenth-century cottages grouped around it as seen in these two views.

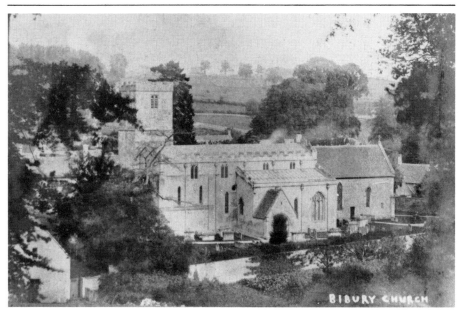

BIBURY CHURCH, c. 1890. The church of St Mary contains work of many periods but still shows much Saxon detail, perhaps suggesting that a large Saxon church existed here which has been continuously altered over the years.

BIBURY COURT, c. 1910. This fine early Jacobean seventeenth-century court stands back behind the church off the road to Coln St Aldwyns. It was built by Thomas Sackville in 1633 with a later addition by Inigo Jones in 1639, but is now an exclusive country hotel.

COLN ST ALDWYNS, c. 1900. This view is to the north across the valley and watermeadows to the church of St John the Baptist. John Keble was vicar here from 1782 to 1835 and his son also followed him as vicar. The gardens across the centre lie alongside the long mill pond leading to Coln Mill.

COLN MILL, c. 1900. Another view across the valley towards the mill and looking up Coln Street. The river crosses the picture in the foreground with the mill race joining to the right. The mill made animal feed and had both water and then steam power – note the chimney.

RED CROSS FIELD DAY AT COLN, 1913. In readiness for the inevitable First World War the Red Cross detachments from the villages held exercises all around the district. This group includes men and women from Fairford, and they practised their medical skills on simulated casualties and also cooked food in the field, often under the fascinated gaze of the villagers.

WILLIAMSTRIP HOUSE, C. 1910. This house is set within the park and was built in the early eighteenth century on a square pattern. It is now the seat of the Hicks-Beach family of the Earl St Aldwyn. In 1946 the left-hand wing was demolished, thereby reducing the house to its original size.

SOCIAL EVENING, 1957.

SOCIAL EVENING, 1958. Local people from around the villages came together to put on small concerts at the village hall in Coln St Aldwyns. Typical acts included singing, dancing, a skiffle group, a comedian and small sketches, all performed with great spirit and giving very good entertainment.

HATHEROP CASTLE, C. 1950. The house is a mid-Victorian rebuild of an old gabled house and was purchased after the work was done by the Bazley family. It is now Hatherop Castle School and this aerial picture shows the castle in the centre, the ornamental Italian gardens to the left at the west end and the rebuilt church of St Nicholas to the right. Above the church are the kitchen gardens and stable block.

WEDDING PARTY AT THE CASTLE, C. 1930. Because Hatherop was largely an estate village any official occasions at the castle almost always involved most of the people in the village. They are gathered here at the main entrance after the marriage of Miss Francis Bazley to author Mr Richard Hughes to watch them leave on their honeymoon.

WELCOME HOME, 1902. An arch was erected over the road to welcome back to Hatherop village Mr Bazley and his wife, the former Miss Howard, after their wedding. On the left is Hatherop School and the three girls standing in the road are Alice Griffin, Mamie Moulden and Beatrice Sims. On the far right is Mr Moulden, the head gardener at the castle.

HATHEROP SCHOOL, 1950. With the children of the school is the headmaster Mr Gwilliam, seated left, and schoolteacher Miss K. Brindle, seated right. Mr Gwilliam was also the organist at the church.

THE VILLAGE CROSS, 1905, with the hunt coming along the street. Note the oil lamp, of which there were about half a dozen around the village. At one time the church sexton used to fill and light them.

GLEBE FARMHOUSE, 1909. At the road junction in the village the finger post points left to Burford and right to Fairford. The large pear tree up the gable-end wall was, and still is, a feature here.

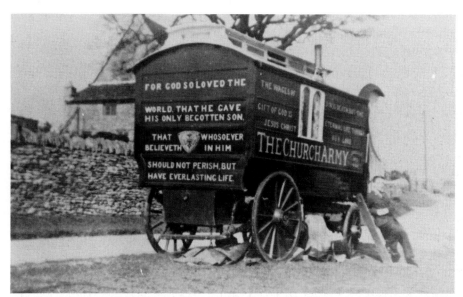

THE CHURCH ARMY, C. 1925. This travelling van, No. 2, based at Cirencester although seen here at Meysey Hampton was known to have made the rounds of most of these Coln valley villages, and memories of it at Hatherop are quite clear. As part of the Church of England they attended various functions in the villages, usually putting up a tent for their religious services.

FRONT STREET AT QUENINGTON, C. 1900. This view shows two of the three pubs here: The Keepers' Arms to the left, the Earl Grey third from left, while the Pig and Whistle, which closed around 1960, was at the top of the village. This road runs down the hill to cross the river just past the church and mill.

QUENINGTON COURT, 1907. On the site of this nineteenth-century house a preceptory of the Knights Hospitallers was founded in 1193. The tall medieval gateway to the court is now the principal remnant.

THE CHURCH, C. 1935. The church of St Swithin has been over-restored but it retains its north and south doorways which are outstanding examples of Norman style. This interior view shows the counterbalanced hanging oil lamp that once graced the church.

QUENINGTON MILL, C. 1930. Next to the church, the mill is thought to have made paper from rags and perhaps this has given the name to Rag Hill up to the left out of the village. The mill used both water and steam power and when the buildings were demolished the chimney was left standing. Mill House is on the right.

CORONATION CELEBRATIONS, 1937. The children of Quenington are seen here holding up their coronation mugs. Sports were also held in the Grandage as part of the celebrations for the crowning of George VI.

QUENINGTON ENTRY IN FAIRFORD CARNIVAL, 1956. Most villages around Fairford entered a float in the carnival and this is the entry of Mrs Wilkins of Quenington School called 'Book of Nursery Rhymes'.

GRANDAGE COTTAGES, C. 1960. These very picturesque cottages stand on their own at the bottom of Fowlers Hill, but until the mid-1960s they had no services except water. Outside is Mr George Burge who worked on the Hatherop Estate and maintained the water-driven turbines that pumped water to Hatherop and Quenington villages. The turbines also operated a 100-volt dynamo that charged large batteries for electrical power to the castle.

THE BULL HOTEL, C. 1900. Advertised as a 'Family and Commercial Hotel', the Bull offered 'Good Stabling and Loose Boxes to let in the Hunting Season and Excellent Trout Fishing' on its two miles of water for 'Dry Fly Fishing Only'. Horse buses, etc. met the trains at the station and daily buses went to Cirencester. Seen here is the local bus that went out around the villages and the Bull Hotel's own bus for use by the guests.

FISHERMEN AT THE BULL HOTEL, 1872. A fine group of Victorian gentlemen ready with their fishing tackle to start the new may fly season. The board above the door shows that Frederick Gibbs was landlord at this time.

THE TOWN BRIDGE, C. 1895. Fishermen often tried their luck in the deep pond below the bridge. Note how the river came out into the roadway here where horses could drink, carts could be washed and traction engines could stop for water. Frederick William Constable, Coach Builders, made wagons, etc. here and the upper floor is stocked with wheels. The works came right out to the edge of the pavement.

OTTER HOUNDS, 1912. These hounds and their followers hunted up and down the River Coln from Fairford to Lechlade, starting or stopping at the Bull Hotel or the New Inn.

THE MILL, C. 1895. The mill was probably being operated by the last miller, Mr Bartlett. The view is very much the same today except that the left-hand gabled end was rebuilt c.1904.

RAF FAIRFORD, 1948. Seen here in the last days prior to closure as a wartime airfield. A visiting Dakota aircraft is here for combined operations with the Horsa gliders being used by 297 Squadron.

FAIRFORD STATION, 1961. The line was opened in 1873 but this picture is from 1961, about one year before closure of the branch line from Witney to Fairford. PT 0–6–0 No. 4649 prepares to take one guards' van up the line! Note the original GWR bench seat and the galvanized iron pagoda-roofed parcels shed, with the station building hidden behind the engine.

TRACTION ENGINE, 1947. Briggs and Rickards kept some of their contract engines and threshing sets in the farmyard opposite the Railway Inn. Here is the Alchin No. 1458 6 hp compound engine DD2006 ready in steam, with the threshing drum sheeted down behind it, on a muddy winter's day in December.

GREAT CLEARANCE SALE, C. 1908. The business of J.W. Russ was transferred to Edgar R. Clifford who held a transfer sale of goods on Friday 27 November. The doors were opened at 10 o'clock and the sale included general drapery, clothing, boots, china, glass, earthenware and ironmongery. The occasion was well advertised with six sandwich boards walking round the town, flags flying and the Fairford Silver Band in attendance.

MARKET PLACE AND HIGH STREET, C. 1870. This is one of the oldest pictures in the selection. On the right is Giles' shop where in 1868 Ellen Giles was a grocer, draper, china, glass and earthenware dealer. James Giles, Boot and Shoe Maker, with a warehouse, was possibly her husband. Looking up the line of shops it can be seen that some present-day buildings are not yet built, such as the former post office and Lloyds Bank, the former Powells, now Hopes' newsagents, and the buildings next to Montacue House.

PARK FARM DAIRY, C. 1900. The milk cart and its gleaming churn are obviously brand new and it has been photographed for the proud owners to use as a postcard and for advertising.

FARMOR'S SCHOOL, 1926. This is Miss Farmer's class and the names from left to right are as follows. Back row: Bill Radway, Jessie Niblet, -?-, Tommy Lawrence, ? Oakey, ? Edney, -?-, -?-. Middle row: -?-, Joyce Nash, Lyla Poole, Ethel Cook, Christine Grant, Lil Thoms, Lettie Hunt, -?-, -?-, -?-, -?-. Front row: Sylvia Honeybone, -?-, Jack Bennett, -?-, Ronnie Groves, Tom Kibblewhite, -?-.

WOMEN'S INSTITUTE, 1929. The WI held some meetings at Fairford Park House by invitation of Mrs Palmer, and members are seen here in a Parade of Shawls. Some of the shawls being worn were reported as being over one hundred years old.

FAIRFORD CARNIVAL, 1914. This was one of the district's greatest shows and it raised funds to support the cottage hospital. Large crowds always gathered in the Market Place to watch the procession go round the streets. In the background is the shop of Herbert Norris, Watchmaker and Dealer in Gold and Silver, while to the right is the shop of R.H. Green, with a warehouse for General Drapery, Fancy Warehouse, Gents Outfitters, Boots and Shoes. It is a hot July Saturday afternoon but there are no concessions to the heat with dresses, suits and hats being worn.

MILTON STREET, C. 1910. The refreshment rooms of W. Cuss were also a cyclists' rest, showing the popularity of cycling in Edwardian times. Townshend's Garage is just about started and Pratt's Motor Spirit is advertised farther on showing that Busby's have taken over from Constable's at the Coach Works. Note the men and boys sitting on the town bridge which was a favourite place to sit and watch the world go by.

CRICKET TEAM, c. 1915. This is thought to be a team representing Fairford Park, who played at the Park Street ground, with names as follows. Back row: Robert Kimber (church sexton), William Andrews (head keeper at park), -?-, Higgins (schoolmaster), Hugh Busby (garage owner), -?-, ? Powell (journeyman at park), Bert Cole. Front row: A. Hitchman Iles, -?-, Sammy Jenkins (police sergeant), -?-, Arthur Derry (head gardener at park).

T.R. STEVENS, BLACKSMITH, c. 1920. Bob Stevens was the blacksmith and also the cycle agent and repairer with his forge in London Street opposite Eastbourne Terrace from 1914–27. He then moved to a shop in Bridge Street, now the post office, and dropped being the blacksmith, selling cycles, motor cycles and petrol.

POPE'S COURT, c. 1900. A meet of the V.W.H. Cricklade Hounds in the field opposite the court. The Thames & Severn Canal feeder from the River Coln below Whelford Mill to Kempsford Wharf used to run round in front of the house as a small shallow ditch.

WHELFORD MILL, C. 1900. A traditional seventeenth-century Cotswold-style building in the flat river plain of the Thames, where slates, pantiles and thatch can be more common than Cotswold stone on the roofs, as will be seen in the following photographs. A horse-drawn wagon is loading by the mill which was the last mill on the River Coln and consequently had plenty of power for its two wheels.

ENTRY IN FAIRFORD CARNIVAL, 1913. E.N. Edmonds, the owner of Whelford Mill, entered this float in the carnival using their sacks of corn and flour on a horse-drawn cart. It was decorated overall in a patriotic manner with Union Jack flags, but note the cart-wheels covered in paper patterns of mill stones.

THE HERMITAGE, 1907. A good photograph of the house which stands next to the church of St Anne's built by G.E. Street in 1863. This picture was a postcard used as a Christmas card by the curate G.H. Kirkham, who is seen here with his wife.

AT COLLETTS BRIDGE, C. 1900. A very peaceful rural scene on the road through from Fairford. Note the pile of broken stone for road mending just by the rails of the bridge over the canal feeder running from Whelford to Kempsford.

THE QUEEN'S HEAD, C. 1900. This was the village pub for Whelford and belonged to Simmonds Brewery up until 1954 when it was pulled down because it was in line with the new runway at RAF Fairford for use by the USAF. In the picture the lady is cutting the reeds that grew along the banks of the canal feeder.

WHERE THE RIVER COLN JOINS THE RIVER THAMES, C. 1930. Here close to Inglesham the Coln is seen flowing into the Thames from beneath the overhanging willow trees in the centre. It has run for more than twenty-five miles from its source and touched upon twenty or so communities. It effectively doubles the flow of the Thames at this junction.

INGLESHAM ROUNDHOUSE AND CANAL JUNCTION, c. 1930. On the corner, just above the point where the two rivers join the Thames, the Thames & Severn Canal also made its junction with the Thames. The canal was opened in 1789 and abandoned in 1927 and it comes under the bridge from its last lock into the river. The footbridge continued the towpath on along the river bank. The roundhouse was where the canal lock-keeper and lengthsman lived and a small warehouse was built alongside to deal with the canal traffic. This soon proved unsuitable and the company bought the established Parkend Wharf at Lechlade.

The Leach Valley Villages

HAMPNETT VILLAGE, C. 1920. This view to the north-east across the valley shows where the Hampnett Brook or River Leach rises. The church of St George in the centre has some interesting late Norman work but was overrestored in 1868 and then subject to excessive painting by the vicar in the 1880s. The open ground is where cattle have grazed for many years and the barns to the right of the church are being converted to houses. Northleach can just be seen in the distance down the valley.

HAMPNETT RECTORY, C. 1935. This large rectory was designed by A.W. Maberly and built in 1872.

THE PUESDOWN INN, C. 1920. This large inn is approximately 2 miles out of Northleach towards Cheltenham along the main road, and is some 850 feet up on the Cotswolds. The landlord Mr Charles Ebborn and his wife are standing outside the inn which offered travellers good accommodation and sold Green's Noted Stout and Sparkling Bitter Ales from the Stow-on-the-Wold Brewery.

THE VICARGE AND CHURCH, C. 1905. This large house built in 1863 is now called Glebe House and is a nursing home. The small mill stream or Wellings Brook flows under the footbridge and into the mill pond of the mill. The church of Saints Peter and Paul was entirely rebuilt in the mid-fifteenth century and is a classic example of the Perpendicular style and a reminder of the wealth of the wool merchants. Inside the church there are many brasses in memory of these merchants.

THE DUTTON ALMSHOUSES, C. 1910. In 1615 Thomas Dutton of Turkdean willed money to build almshouses in Northleach and they were built in East End. Originally six, but now altered to four to make them bigger inside, they are administered by the town trustees.

THE PRISON, C. 1910. This House of Correction was opened in 1791 to attempt to improve prison conditions. But this picture portrays a forbidding building which has now been altered to house the Cotswold Countryside Collection, a museum of rural life. In this view the left-hand section was the police station and the delivery van of George Giles, who traded from Northleach Market Place as a corn, flour and meal factor, is seen entering the yard from the prison crossroads.

WEST END, 1913. This is the approach road down into Northleach with the iron gates of the brewery on the left. By the tree on the right is the Cotswold Hall built in 1894 on the site of an old row of cottages. It was for the use of the town people and upstairs was a large hall for dances and other functions, while downstairs was a billiards room, a room for the vicar and the caretaker's accommodation. The infant River Leach is culverted under the road along here.

THE MARKET PLACE, C. 1910.

THE MARKET PLACE, C. 1930. On the left in the top view of these two similar pictures of the north side of the Market Place is F.W. Gardiner's shop and Northleach Press, with the Union Hotel farther down. Note the large double telegraph poles that were erected along the A40 and through the town in 1907. In the lower view is the war memorial which was unveiled in 1922 and the shop of J.A. Hills on the left who sold cycles and petrol, etc.

THE MARKET PLACE, c. 1910.

THE MARKET PLACE, c. 1920. Again two more similar pictures of a different view of the Market Place and some of the sixteenth- and seventeenth-century buildings that surround it. In the top view from left to right is the Sherborne Arms, the Isle (now Lloyds Bank), the Woolhouse, the church in the background, the Old Lock Up, Burges sweet shop, the post office, the previous site of the bank and then, continuing to the lower picture, is Eltome's grocers shop and finally Bartlett's the Chemist. The small River Leach is culverted under the Market Place, and the Union Hotel sign is on the grass island where the bus shelter and toilets were built in 1961.

EASTINGTON VILLAGE, C. 1950. Here in the garden of Eastington Cottage the small River Leach tumbles on its way down towards Lodge Park which was built around 1650 by John Dutton and was where people could watch deer-coursing events in the surrounding park. It was altered to a house in 1898.

EASTINGTON CHURCH, C. 1960. A mid-Victorian building which was formerly the village school, but is now converted to a house.

ALDSWORTH, C. 1930. The road from Cirencester to Burford is shown as the B4425 on the finger posts and runs across the picture while the road into the village goes up through to Northleach. The village is off the main road and about a mile north of the River Leach valley. Note the chapel up on the bank and the houses in the front. The first on the right was the school house with the reading room attached to it, and the post office was in the centre of the row.

ALDSWORTH FROM THE BURFORD ROAD, C. 1905. This small lane and footpath led up into the village from the main road to Legg's Bakery. The lady and children are probably waiting for the horse bus to take them into Cirencester.

ALDSWORTH VILLAGE, C. 1930. This view is looking up the lane into the village where Cecil Collett the blacksmith had his forge and did repair jobs on carts and farm machinery, and these await repair in the lane.

THE FAIRY WELL, ALDSWORTH, C. 1930. Water is being dipped out of the well in buckets to fill the horse-drawn water tank which took water round the houses and farms before a supply of water was laid on from Bibury.

THE CHOIR OF ST BARTHOLOMEW'S CHURCH, ALDSWORTH, 1925. This church is late Norman with a considerable amount of Perpendicular work. This picture has the vicar Revd Hay in the centre of the middle row and the choirmaster Mr Lambert is on the left of the middle row.

ALDSWORTH SCHOOL, c. 1900. A typical late Victorian school photograph. The schoolmaster can just be seen to the left and the two schoolmistresses to the right. The building has now been converted into a house.

DEAN FARM, C. 1955. This house was built in 1897 in the Cotswold style and is the home of Lord Howard of Penrith. Just to the north is Dean Camp, an Iron Age hill-fort enclosing about ten acres. After the River Leach has left Northleach and Eastington it only touches upon three isolated farms in the next ten miles until it reaches Eastleach. These three farms are Kilkenny, Swyre and Dean Farm.

NON-CONFORMIST MEETING AT DEAN FARM, 1907. This is thought to be the Fairford Chapel Treat which was held at Dean Farm on 1 August. There were reported to be over three hundred people at the event which must have included chapel people from all over the district, although they are not all included on this photograph.

EASTLEACH MARTIN CHURCH, 1819. This is from a pencil drawing of the church of Saints Michael and Martin otherwise known as Bouthrop church. It is by Miss Alice Keble, the sister of John Keble who ministered here from 1815 for eight years. The age of the stone clapper bridge across the River Leach called Keble's Bridge is unknown but could well be many hundreds of years. This church is no longer used but is maintained by the Redundant Churches Fund, and it is a pretty church with its hipped tower roof, having been founded in early Norman days.

EASTLEACH RECTORY, C. 1905. Built in C. 1700 but now much altered, the rectory is seen here on a winter's day with the postman Alf Berry struggling through the snow. The view is almost unchanged today.

THE SWORD DANCING TEAM, 1932/3. The team is assembled on the school bank. They took part in local dancing festivals and the two boys are holding the banners from the Witney District Musical Festival, while three girls are holding framed certificates.

VIEWS AROUND THE VILLAGE, C.1925. This was a common way of producing a postcard for villages. Clockwise the views are Eastleach Turville, the bridge over the river, Back Street, Middle Street and the oval centre is Bouthrop church.

CAUSEY BARN, C. 1940. Originally this was four cottages, but is now one house. Keble Bridge is in the foreground with the steps down to the water broken away badly. People dipped buckets for their water from these steps before the water supply was installed.

BRIDGE COTTAGE, 1934. A delightful rural scene looking towards the church of St Andrew with its fourteenth-century saddle-backed tower. Bridge Cottage was once a small shop and is the first house in Eastleach Turville after crossing the bridge.

PRIMITIVE METHODIST CHAPEL, 1909. The chapel was built and finally finished by November 1909 and had a fairly strong following from the surrounding villages. It is shown here newly finished with gleaming quoin-work, but has now been converted into a house.

OXEN AT WORK, C. 1905. A team of four oxen ploughing land at Crabtree Bottom between Eastleach Turville and Southrop. The leading oxen is guided by a young boy but the plough is held by an old experienced ploughman. It is said that four oxen pulled the plough slowly but steadily.

A SCHOOL CELEBRATION. The occasion is not known but the dancing could have been for all sorts of celebrations, such as May Day, a coronation, or the end of the First World War, since the few boys in the picture do have a military style about them. They are outside the post office, which the notice tells us handled money orders, savings bank, parcel post and insurance.

AGRICULTURAL WORKERS' MEETING, C. 1905. Dissatisfaction with low pay and long hours led to disturbances among farm workers and meetings were held in the villages. Here in Eastleach the local band is helping the occasion along at the bottom of Pudding Hill. Note the oil lamp on this corner.

ROGATION DAY, 1929. This is the parade over Keble's Bridge and around the village to seek God's blessing for agriculture. The parades are based on old rituals that attempted to keep crops free of disease and animals fertile. Canon Wright, the Rector of Eastleach, is second from right.

RAF SOUTHROP VS. EASTLEACH FOOTBALL MATCH, 1944. The match was played at Southrop and in the centre is Air Marshall Cassidy holding the ball. Unfortunately the names of the RAF team to the left are not known but the Eastleach team in the hooped shirts is as follows. Back row: J. Tovey, A. Preston, A. Hobbs, F. Watcutt, B. Clack, A. Pitts, referee. Front row: C. Puffett, T. Atkins, R. Sims, B. Berry, R. Hatton.

BRINGING HOME THE RABBITS, 1956. Mr Jack Tovey is seen here with the results of a good Sunday morning's rabbiting trip. He often cycled into Circencester to sell them to Charles Barnett's game shop in the Market Place.

THE VICARAGE, C. 1905. Also known as Southrop Lodge this was the home of John Keble while he was curate at the church of St Peter. It is believed that much of his work *The Christian Year* was written here, perhaps under the large cedar tree to the right. The church shows a good deal of Norman work and the thirteenth-century font is outstanding.

THE GREEN, C. 1920. A typical Cotswold scene along the road through the village from Fairford. The village hall is off to the left and the present Dalgety concern is at the end between the remaining cottages.

THE POST OFFICE, C. 1920. Most villages had a post office of this type usually combined with a grocery shop. The village telephone was here and outside there are advertisements for Home and Colonial tea, Lyons tea, Gold Flake and Brownie tobaccos. The shop was probably run by Telling.

OTTER HOUNDS AT THE SWAN, c. 1915.

THE SWAN, c. 1915. The pub was one of the centres of village life and in the top view the otter hounds and their followers are meeting prior to hunting down the River Leach to Lechlade, while in the lower view the wife of the landlord George Newman stands in the doorway as a group of children and other passers-by are posed by the photographer for the occasion.

SOUTHROP SCHOOL, c. 1910. The school buildings are off to the left and the maypole is in the playground at the back. The occasion is unclear but it is possibly a May Day, Empire Day or coronation celebration.

VIEWS AROUND THE VILLAGE, c. 1925. A similar postcard to that of Eastleach. From the top left the scenes are the post office, a street scene, the Swan, a street scene and the centre oval is the Manor House.

SOUTHROP CHURCH, c. 1920. The small church of St Peter is early Norman and herring-bone masonry and an original window can be seen in the wall of the church. John Keble was curate here from 1823 to 1825 and it is thought that he discovered the twelfth-century font that had been built into a doorway in the church. The font is one of the finest Norman remains in the Cotswold district.

MANOR HOUSE, 1902. Interestingly the house standing next to the church has a Norman doorway and chevron moulding round it. Mr Thomas Arkell and his family are standing on the lawn. The estate comprised some 1200 acres needing eighteen horses, twelve oxen for ploughing, and employing thirty-two farm workers and two shepherds.

HARVESTING SCENE AT MANOR FARM, C. 1910. It is immediately apparent from this picture what a big operation harvesting was on a large farm in the days of horsepower. Three binders have been used to cut the corn which has been stooked to ripen and dry in the field almost as far as can be seen. Two ricks have already been built and thatched ready for winter, and about twenty people have been involved.

OXEN READY FOR WORK AT MANOR FARM, c. 1910.

LARGE OXEN TEAM AT MANOR FARM, c. 1910. In the top picture three oxen are harnessed to a single furrow plough, while in the lower picture six oxen are harnessed together near Prices Barn ready for a much heavier task and needing two boys to lead them.

THE RIVER LEACH AT LITTLE FARINGDON, C. 1915. This is the river looking upstream towards Southrop from the road bridge between Lechlade and Burford. The county boundary between Gloucestershire and Oxfordshire lies along the river just above here and Little Faringdon is in Oxfordshire.

LITTLE FARINGDON MILL, C. 1910. This is the view of the mill looking downstream from the main road. It was worked up to the 1960s and the last miller was Harold Lock. It has been restored in recent years and the grounds are now a trout farm.

LITTLE FARINGDON CHURCH, c. 1930. This small Norman church has no dedication and has been altered over the centuries.

LITTLE FARINGDON LEVEL CROSSING, 1914. The road from the village to Kelmscott was crossed by the railway in 1873 and guarded by this level crossing where a house was built for the crossing keeper. Note the two oil lamps here to light this isolated location.

LITTLE FARINGDON HOUSE, c. 1910. The house in this picture was the residence of Lord De Mauley and was otherwise known as Langford House. Lying to the north-west of the church it was built in the seventeenth century and enlarged in the eighteenth century while the castellated front and the Tudor-style windows were added in 1820.

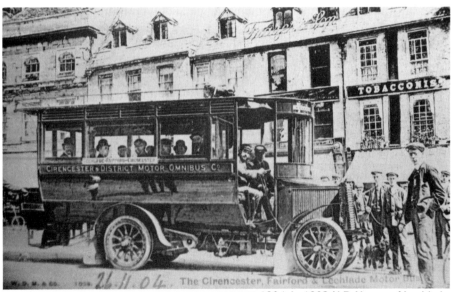

THE CIRENCESTER, FAIRFORD AND LECHLADE MOTOR BUS, 1904. In 1903 M.R. Young of Lechlade put into service two Clarkson steam buses AD303 and AD304, to operate twice a day between Lechlade and Cirencester. The 13-mile journey took between 1 hour 15 minutes and 1 hour 40 minutes and the bus is seen here in Cirencester Market Place. They did not prove successful and were replaced after a few years by horse buses.

THE RIVER THAMES, C. 1930. Looking down the river to Parkend Wharf, which was bought by the Thames & Severn Canal Company in 1813. When canal and river traffic ceased the wharf became the base for several leisure activities and the long tin-roofed shed was put up to shelter the hire boats of which a typical one is seen here. Half Penny Pike Bridge to the right was built in 1792 for the road to Highworth and Swindon.

VIEW FROM THE CHURCH TOWER, 1914. From this view can be seen the wharf, the river upstream and the clump of poplar trees which marks the canal junction. On the wharf are bundles of reeds cut higher up the river and canal and ready to be sent down the river for furniture seats. The coal on the wharf has probably been sent down the Oxford Canal and up the river as the Thames & Severn Canal had ceased trading by this date.

PARKEND WHARF, 1903.

GEORGE J. HICKS' ADVERTISEMENT, 1903. George took over the wharf from his father Matthew and the top picture shows the wharf from the Highworth Road with his name on the shed. The lower picture shows a typical advertisement of the day for the services to be found at the wharf, but note the GWR Lechlade station mentioned for coal and coke, as opposed to that brought down the canals and river.

PARKEND WHARF, C. 1890. This is a good working picture of the wharf. To the left is the tail end of a Matthew Hicks coal barge and the warehouse behind it. A cart shed is in the centre by the wharf entrance off Thames Street, and stone lies on the wharf by the side arm. It is also interesting to see how the centre of Lechlade is built on slightly higher ground up from the level of the river.

THE SCHOOL, 1908. There were three schools in this area behind the church and these children could be from any one, but most likely they are from the Grey Gable private school in the house to the right. The low house to the left, Caxton House, was where the schoolmaster of St Lawrence's school lived.

WATER CARNIVAL, 1906. A carnival was held on the river from 1903 to 1935 on August Bank Holiday each year. All events were to do with the river and included swimming, diving, canoeing, decorated punts and barrel racing, etc. Side shows were in the meadow alongside the south bank of the river and this large Edwardian crowd is assembled in the grounds of the New Inn meadow which was an excellent vantage point from which to watch the carnival.

CLAYDON FARM, c. 1920. C.B. Metcalfe had an egg farm at Claydon, mid-way between Lechlade and Fairford and he used this International lorry AD7238 to take the boxes of eggs to the local markets or to the station.

LECHLADE STATION, 1961.

LECHLADE STATION, 1961. The branch line was opened in 1873 and these two pictures are taken about one year before closure in June 1962. The station was almost a mile from the town to the north and the top view is taken from the bridge over the line taking the road from Lechlade to Burford and shows the complete station layout looking towards Oxford. The lower view shows PT 0–6–0 No. 3722 leaving the station for Oxford.

THE SHOEMENDER, c. 1930. Ted Blackwell is 'shoe snobbing' in Sherborne Street. Note the lion tap in the background, of which there were many round the streets of Lechlade, which supplied the water.

GILLETT'S SHOP, 1930. A proud day for manager Mr George Morley as Gillett's new grocery shop is opened in Lechlade Market Place, next to Lloyds Bank. Shop assistant Dean stands to the left, and delivery boy Taylor with the carrier bicycle.

LECHLADE MARKET. A crowded and busy scene at the new Lechlade Livestock Market adjacent to the railway line by the Burford Road bridge. The market moved to this purpose-built site from the streets and Market Place.

Downington, Lechlade.

BRIDGE HOUSE, DOWNINGTON, C. 1930. The Wurn Brook runs out from Butlers Court Farm, alongside the road into Lechlade and then under the bridge to join the Thames. Bowly the builder was here with his yard and saw mill at the rear; note his stock of chimney pots on the wall to the left.

VWH HORSE SHOW,1909. This show was held at Butlers Court Farm and included horse judging, racing and jumping, somewhat similar to present day Point-to-Point events. There appears to be a good following and many people have travelled to the show in cars which are lined up at the back.

CORONATION DECORATIONS, 1911. The Market Place was decorated with bunting and the shops all have flags out for the occasion in June. The post office on the right has a banner out proclaiming 'God Save The King'.

LECHLADE CHURCH, 1908. This view of St Lawrence's church shows a policeman standing outside the police station with the shop of C.J. Higgs, Breeches Maker, next to the church. The church is a fine example of late Perpendicular style, built in 1476. The hexagonal spire is very prominent and an excellent landmark for miles around in the flat countryside of the River Thames plain.

HORSE FAIR, 1913. Lechlade Horse Fair was a big occasion with many horses being offered for sale. The horses were tethered along a rail against the wall up Oak Street and Burford Road. Also for sale were sets of harness, carts and tools, etc.

LECHLADE FAIR, 1913. Held on 9 September each year, a fun fair fills the Market Place and Burford Road in this view taken from a window of the New Inn. All the vans are horse drawn, but the big roundabout to the front right has a chimney through the centre of the canvas roof as it is steam powered. It is thought that the fair derived from an earlier hiring fair.

PEACE CELEBRATIONS, 1919.

PEACE CELEBRATIONS, 1919. A peace parade was held to celebrate the end of the First World War. In the top picture decorated horse floats and boy scouts are shown in the parade outside the New Inn, while in the lower picture a few flags are flying as people pose in their doorways in Thames Street with the Half Penny Pike Bridge in the background.

FOOTBALL TEAM, 1912/13. Lechlade Football Club taken in the front garden of Davis the Chemist, the professional photographer for the district. The coach arch of the New Inn is seen across the Market Place.

ST JOHN'S LOCK, C. 1900. This is the first lock on the River Thames and was built in 1873. The lockhouse is to the left and the whole scene looks very neat and tidy. The original lockhouse was on the opposite side of the lock behind the trees.

THE TROUT INN, 1907. This building is one of the oldest pubs in the district and it is thought that a building has stood here since c.1200. St John's Bridge over the river here was built in 1229 close by the Priory of St John. Mr J. Bowyer the landlord is standing outside and Bowlys' Entire was the beer supplied by the Brewery at Stratton St Margaret, Swindon. At this bridge the four counties of Gloucestershire, Oxfordshire, Wiltshire and Berkshire all used to meet until the county boundary of Oxfordshire was extended to the south in 1974.

THE WEIR AT ST JOHN'S LOCK, c. 1930. Seen here is the manually-operated weir across the river adjacent to the lock. Originally the site was a flash weir which was just opened to allow barges and boats through on a rush of water. In the background is the Trout Inn with its gardens down to the river bank.

THE TROUT INN MEADOW, 1939. Looking down the river from the bridge, these chalets belonged to the Trout and could be hired as holiday homes. It was possible to swim in the wide and deep part of the river in the foreground and a ladder was provided to climb out on. The junction of the River Leach with the Thames is in the background as the Leach enters from the left.

ACKNOWLEDGEMENTS

In general, most of the photographs shown in this selection were originally taken by the local professional photographers who used to travel round their districts recording the events taking place and the scenes in the villages. They covered the period from mid-Victorian times through to the 1940s and undoubtedly without their efforts we would not have been able to make such a selection. Thankfully a great deal of their work survives, mainly as postcards, upon which our own collections of photographs are based, but sadly much of their work must now be lost after the passing of 50 to 100 years.

The list of these photographers includes:

W. Butt of Bourton-on-the-Water
Davis of Lechlade
J.W. Gardner of Fairford
Hooper of Swindon
M. Savory and W. Dennis Moss of Cirencester
T. Musto of Bibury
C. Powell and A. Powell of Fairford
P. Simms and F. Packer of Chipping Norton
H. Stokes of Andoversford
H. Taunt of Oxford

Some of the photographs we have used have no names on them and others are the invaluable snapshots taken by people in the days when small box cameras came into use. We hope that from whatever source they come that they all add up to an interesting 'peep' back into the past, to use one of the favourite words of W. Dennis Moss, the professional photographer of Cirencester to whom we are especially indebted.

We would, therefore, like to thank all those people who have so willingly helped us by loaning photographs and especially those who gave us information and their help is duly acknowledged below:

Mrs M. Bradley • Mrs and Mrs G. Burge • Canal Card Collectors Circle
Cotswold Postcard Collectors Club • Mr S. Flatman • Mrs Gardiner
Mr A.N. Irvine • Mrs S. Lovesey • Mr G. Morley • Mr D. Perry • Mr B. Rushby
Mr R. Sims • Mr P. Strong • Miss E. Sly • Miss A. Tremaine • Mr. D. Viner.